All Scripture references taken from the KJV
of the Holy Bible, unless otherwise indicated.

SLAVE by Dr. Marlene Miles

Freshwater Press 2025

Freshwaterpress9@gmail.com

ISBN: 978-1-967860-18-0

Paperback Version

Table of Contents

SLAVE

Freshwater

Introduction

This is a troubling book. I had no idea it would be this disturbing when starting because I was only looking at a simple problem that seems to be either the remaining vestiges of a serious global epidemic, or it could be the beginning of the entire problem of slavery. I don't know if what I intended to write is the beginning or the end of something so heinous. I also don't know if there is an end, in the natural, or that this problem might be circular due the evil in the hearts of men.

There is hope, though. There is one end to it and that is Jesus Christ.

Getting Paid

This book is for everyone who works but doesn't get paid. It is for those who work but don't get paid what they are supposed to get. This message is for those who work at the same place and doing the same work as others, but the others seem to get more than you do.

The *spirit of the slave* may be on you and today we need to pray it off of you, in the Name of Jesus.

Every civilization that grew to be a kingdom or an empire had slaves. That doesn't make it right. Every people group has been enslaved at some time or other and sometimes by their own people. That does not make any people group a perpetual victim. Some people are so passive that they don't try to get out of enslavement if they are ever found in it.

The *spirit of the slave* is a real thing. If a person doesn't know who he or she is, they could end up anywhere and in anything.

I ask any of us again, are we enslaved? Are we enslaved by the system? By the laws of the land we live in? Are we enslaved by the choice of work that we do? Have the **GATES** of that particular job that you do not opened to you? Have you forced your way in? Have you felt as though you had to force your way in? You wanted to be an engineer so badly, but everything has been a struggle? Not because you can't do it, not because you don't have credentials, but the culture you live and work in are blocking or prohibiting you? The systems that are in place make you a slave, earning far less than the other "engineers" in your same field?

An architect I know was awesome, educated in one of the most prestigious schools in the world, but why did he not end up successful?

You've met some who are successful and in the same field, but another is not.

Why?

It is spiritual.

1. Did God agree that this is what you should be doing in your career? Yes? Well, amen.
2. Are you serving the Lord, faithfully? Amen.
3. Are you *all in Christ* or just hanging around the edges of when and where you got saved?

Yes, to all of those questions? Then command the Gates of that profession to open up to you. if you haven't done it since you chose that profession, command it (Psalm 24). Oh, women don't do that job.

Lift up ye heads, O ye Gates. Amen.

If you've been told that women aren't plumbers or can't do this or that, but you know God told you to do it, or at least okayed it, then command the gates to open to you for the career that you are called to do and do that job. People of a certain background don't do this? Command the gates to open to you, in the Name of Jesus.

Lift up ye heads, O ye Gates. Amen.

Sin has bondage, so if you are not all in Christ then the residual, the smoke of sin may still be on you and bondage you know is enslavement—it could be that smoke that is on a person as to why they are enslaved.

Slaves often have self-esteem issues, a man ought not to think more of himself than he ought, but he shouldn't think less of himself either. A slave who thinks they can <u>earn</u> their way out of slavery is the **perfect slave.** That person will remain a slave. Even in families. We are not saved by **works**. (Not speaking of indentured servanthood or serfdom here.)

Similarly, the person who thinks they can do enough good works to earn their way into Heaven or at least not go to hell, is mistaken. We are not saved by works; **we are saved by GRACE, and it is a gift of GOD.** The person who thinks they can do enough to please whoever is lording over them or trying to be a master over them is deceived, we are not saved by works.

The spouse who thinks if they do this one more thing or this one more thing a certain way then their abusive spouse will love them: **WE ARE NOT SAVED BY WORKS**.

The parents who think if they give their child one more expensive gift they will stop being lazy, go to school, and stop slacking off and partying.

It's NOT BY WORKS.

To the enslaved person, even if you are enslaved to your own family: **We Are Not Saved By Works.**

Sometimes the slave of the family is the parent or the parents. Have they made themselves into slaves, thinking it is love? We cannot buy love. If you set yourself up as your child's slave, when and where and how will they learn anything else?

God loves and will reward the diligent, but we are not saved by works. It is by the Grace of God, by His Mercy and lovingkindness. It is by the Spirit of God that we are set free and fully redeemed from the Curse of the law. It is by the Blood of Jesus that we are redeemed back to the Father.

So, keep working. Keep doing the same thing and expecting a different result. It won't happen. Nothing will change until you address it spiritually.

Back to the workforce—or even school: The person who has to work **twice as hard for any recognition** or promotion to level the field when they see others are having it so easy; it may be that your works won't be acknowledged or rewarded after all. WE ARE NOT SAVED BY WORKS: Get the *spirit of the slave* off of you. and you must do that spiritually.

(Book: **Level the Playing Field** by this author: https://a.co/d/7OPc12q)

How to Build an Empire

Few if any empires or great kingdoms have ever been built without slaves or forced labor. That is an indictment upon humanity, but history is history. We will not be focusing on slavery throughout history, but it will be mentioned. This book will talk about individuals as slaves, even in free society. Even in a free family, one, or more--, if there is familial slavery in a family – there isn't always. But if it is present, usually one family member is chosen and treated as a slave or the work horse of the family.

Approximately 30 kingdoms had slaves or forced labor. These kingdoms and empires were **undeniably powerful and wealthy** in their time, with influence beyond their borders. They were recognized for their substantial wealth, territorial dominance, military strength, and or cultural legacy.

Work forms the economic background of a nation or a kingdom or empire. To be king over a kingdom where people either don't work or don't work regularly is a disaster. In ancient empires: slaves worked in agriculture, construction, households, and mines.

Kingdoms or empires where slavery or forced labor was integral to their rise are listed below.

Ancient Era

Ancient Egypt used forced labor, though not always chattel slavery in projects such as the pyramids.

Sumerian City-States had debt slavery and war captives.

Akkadian Empire enslaved conquered peoples, a common Mesopotamian practice.

Babylonian Empire had widespread institutional slavery.

Hittite Empire enslaved war captives for farming and construction.

Assyrian Empire –Brutally used war captive slaves.

Persian Achaemenid Empire (c. 550–330 BCE)

Macedonian Empire

Maurya Empire
Han Dynasty (China)

Classical to Medieval Period

Roman Empire
Byzantine Empire
Gupta Empire
Sassanid Empire
Tang Dynasty
Abbasid Caliphate enslaved African and Turks, used in farms, armies, and palaces.

Umayyad Caliphate enslaved captured peoples. Slavery was widespread in the Islamic world.

Holy Roman Empire - Serfdom, a form of semi-slavery, was common.

Ghana Empire -Traded slaves across the Sahara and within its territories.

Mali Empire -Mansa Musa's empire; slavery was institutional.

Song Dynasty- Had slaves and used forced labor.

Mongol Empire -massive use of enslaved peoples from conquered regions, across Eurasia.

Aztec Empire - Slavery was fulfilled by war captives, criminal punishment).

Inca Empire - Used *mit'a* system — forced labor for the state. Technically not slavery, but extremely similar.

In colonial empires: slaves powered cash crops (sugar, cotton, tobacco) that made European nations rich.

Early Modern to Modern Era

Ottoman Empire -Slaves made up the sultan's guard, concubines and domestic slaves.

Mughal Empire - Slavery was common.

Spanish Empire enslaved Indigenous peoples, then Africans in the Americas — key to colonial wealth.

Portuguese Empire – major driver of the transatlantic slave trade.

British Empire - Transatlantic slave trade; slave labor fueled Caribbean and American wealth.

French Colonial Empire -Deeply involved in the slave trade and plantation economy of Haiti, and others islands.

Qing Dynasty – Domestic and rural slavery. They also used corvée labor.

Russian Empire – Used serfdom (a form of hereditary servitude) until 1861. Used slavery in earlier centuries.

In summary, out of 32 kingdoms and empires, they all used slavery or forced labor significantly. Slavery or forced labor was a near-universal feature of powerful empires before the modern era. Whether as war captives, debt slaves, serfs, or forced laborers, the subjugation of human beings was a tragic but central part of building wealth and empires for most of recorded history.

Slavery was so common in empire-building because labor equals wealth. Before machines, human labor was the engine of productivity. To build cities, roads, temples, or run economies, rulers needed large, cheap (or free) workforces. Enslaving people was the most brutally efficient way to do that.

Most empires expanded through conquest. Capturing and enslaving defeated populations was considered normal, even honorable. The bigger the empire, the more captives, and slaves. Slavery reinforced elite power. It created a visible, permanent underclass that reminded everyone who ruled. In many cultures, having slaves was a status symbol.

Sadly, slavery was often justified by religion, law, or culture — whether it was the Roman idea of *natural slavery*, Islamic legal codes, or European racial theories, later on.

What does this have to do with anything? Well, people do what they see others do. People often do what has been done to them. Hurting people hurt people. People also are prone to idolatry and in idolizing one group, they may demonize or marginalize another people group even to the point of enslaving them.

Even when formal slavery declined, other forms of servitude took its place.

- Serfdom (medieval Europe, Russia)
- Corvée labor (China, Inca Empire, France) – mandatory public labor.
- Indentured servitude (colonial America, Caribbean) – contractually bound labor, often brutal.
- Debt peonage, caste-based labor, and forced colonial labor also filled similar roles.

Never Been Enslaved

Very, very few (if any) people groups have *never* experienced slavery or collective subjugation in some form throughout history. When a people group or ethnic group has **never** had **any portion** of its population enslaved at any point in history — through war, conquest, trade, colonization, or internal systems., we can say they've never been enslaved. Then the number of such groups is likely **zero** or **so small and isolated** as to be extremely rare and difficult to verify.

Everyone has been enslaved at some point since slavery was global, and it was an ancient practice. Every major civilization-- African, European, Asian, Indigenous American, Pacific Islander — practiced some form of slavery or servitude.

Even powerful groups were enslaved. Romans enslaved other Romans. Africans enslaved other Africans. Arabs enslaved Turks and vice versa. Slavery wasn't always about race, it was about power and war and money.

Isolation helped people groups to escape ever having been enslaved, but it does not equate to immunity in avoiding being enslaved and remaining free. . Some isolated tribes have been subject to raids or colonization. And even if not captured by outsiders, many had internal servitude systems such as debt slavery, and caste-based roles.

There may be only a few groups *who may have totally escaped being enslaved collectively. Such may be the case of* Isolated hunter-gatherer tribes such as the Sentinelese of the Andaman Islands. Total isolation for millennia. No evidence of contact, conquest, or slavery. But this is because they violently repelled outsiders — and we know very little about them internally.

Some Arctic indigenous groups such as Inuit, Chukchi were remote and mobile. Less likely to be targets of enslavement. However, some contact with Russians and others may have included forced labor.

Isolation may have been their saving grace from remote mountain or jungle people such as Papuan tribes and Amazonian people being captured and made into slaves.

Still, these are exceptions due to remoteness, not because they were inherently immune to slavery. Sad, but if they could get their hands on some slaves, they would have had slaves.

Sadly, it seems that men like slaves if they are the slave owner and they are the ones being served or enriched. Some of our modern-day "slaves" are devices and appliances that do our bidding--, stoves, ovens, Alexa, TV remotes and et cetera. Machines and robots are for the purpose of replacing humans but still provide services that a person pays one time for, little for, or never pays for. My point is: it is built in to the average man to either be king, want to be king, and be served.

Is something wrong with us?

What is it about us that makes us want to think higher of ourselves than we ought and to think less of others? And also, what is it in a man, or what has been taken out of a man that creates the condition for him to become a slave? Or, to remain a slave.

If that man is not in Christ, Set apart and having the Mind of Christ, he can be overcome, manipulated, coerced, or tricked to become a slave and sometimes not even fight against it. Just as the slave owner thinks more of himself than he should, perhaps the slave thinks far less of himself than he should. The knee should be bent to God only, and not to any idol or man. This does not mean to disrespect natural governments, authority, or order, but we don't worship anyone; only God.

Jesus said: The prince of this world cometh, and he has nothing in me. The prince of this world is seeking worship; he tried to trick or entice Jesus into just that in the Wilderness Temptations, but Jesus wasn't buying it. Jesus was not ever enslaved. Old Testament Christ types were enslaved, by force, (Joseph) and by collective captivity (Daniel), for example.

The devil had nothing in Jesus, nothing against Him so He could not be captured or enslaved. Further evidence of this is that in the Bible, many times guilty parties are often stoned. Jesus was never stoned, although they attempted it.

There are a few instances in the Bible where people attempted to stone Jesus. These events are recorded in the Gospel of John:

At this, they picked up stones to stone him, but Jesus hid himself, slipping away from the temple grounds. (John 8:59)

This occurred after Jesus declared, *"Before Abraham was, I am."* (John 8:58), which the people understood as a claim to divinity. A man invoking the divine name, "I AM" (Yahweh), was considered blasphemous by Jewish leaders.

Again his Jewish opponents picked up stones to stone him, but Jesus said to them, 'I have shown you many good works from the Father. For which of these do you stone me?' They replied, 'We are not stoning you for any good work,' they replied, 'but for blasphemy, because you, a mere man, claim to be God. (John 10:31-33)

This happened after Jesus said, *"I and the Father are one,"* (John 10:30), which was a claim to divinity that the religious leaders considered blasphemy.

In both cases, the attempt to stone Jesus was based on the accusation of **blasphemy**, as claiming to be God was a capital offense under Jewish law (see Leviticus 24:16).

The stone? Let he who is without sin cast the first stone (John 8:7).

The devil sinned, that is how he got kicked out of Heaven, and he has been trying to put up stones of offence and stumbling blocks for mankind ever since. There is no redemption for the devil, but Jesus has come to redeem mankind back to the Father. Amen.

But they couldn't stone Him. There was nothing in Him to allow anyone to do anything at all to Him, unless He allowed it and they broke spiritual law. And both those things happened, in the end.

Most Enslaved

- **Slavs** (origin of the word "slave")

- **Africans** -millions via transatlantic and Islamic trades.

- **Arabs** -enslaved by Mongols and intertribal wars.

- **Chinese** -under Mongols, and internal dynastic wars.

- **Greeks** -enslaved by Romans, Persians, Turks.

- **Irish** (indentured and enslaved during English colonization)

- **Indigenous Americans** – enslaved by Aztecs, Incas, then Europeans.

- **Jews** were enslaved in Egypt, Babylon, Rome, and Nazi Europe.

- **Pacific Islanders** Black birding was the name for kidnapping 19th-century, Pacific Islanders to slave on plantations.

- **South Asians** - enslaved within caste system and under Muslim, British empires.

Almost no group of people in human history has completely escaped enslavement, either as victims of external forces or through internal servitude.

Because of the history of slavery throughout the world, over centuries, people have learned strange things, such as having servants and having people to serve them. People want things made easy or easier for them. When the *spirit of slavery* gets in a people, they are more prone to become slaves. Conversely when the *spirit of the master* comes upon a people they think they deserve slaves and should have them.

Caste systems come into play where through some physical trait usually, people decide that they are better than others, or those who don't measure up end up feeling like they are less than others, and everyone "knows their place," and simply falls in position. In one Hispanic family, one family member is constantly telling the others that she is better than they are, or better looking because her skin is lighter. She believes it herself and through constant propaganda, they may too. But as of now, they haven't, they push back on her foolishness. She wants to create a caste system in her family.

It's not like that in God. It's not like that in the Kingdom of Heaven. God is no respecter of persons.

The guy that comes into the kingdom first is "paid" the same as the guy who comes in at the 11th hour. Everyone is treated the same. There is equity, and there is justice and dignity for all.

But because of human nature, some do want to lord themselves over others and some feel entitled to do so. Others, cower back or are super humble and with an untempered Gift of Helps, By that I mean the Holy Spirit is not actively directing and measuring out this gift. Many times, people take the Gift of Helps to be weakness. It is not; it is a powerful gift of God.

Without salvation and true repentance and absolution from sin, a person could feel guilty. And if they are not saved, they may believe that by works they can be loved, or forgiven, or become good enough for those disdainful ones who believe they are perfect, and their "subjects" are not.

Assimilators, *wake up*.

Then there are the greedy souls who want everything they see and everything they imagine. They also want everything that another person has, even their life. They won't kill the person, but they want to, like a vampire, suck the life and all the goodness out of another person's life. These are the makings of users and takers, and wanna-be slave masters.

These are the types that want buildings built and their names put on those buildings. These are the types who want everything on such a grand scale that they must use hundreds of people to build something that is great enough for them. These are the types who would as soon dispose of those who do not do their bidding, or dispose of them once they are done with them and have used them up. These are Haman types who said, "Who better to honor than me?"

Spiritual Slavery

You may ask, what does any of this have to do with me? Maybe nothing, maybe everything.

Spiritual slavery refers to the condition of being bound or enslaved by sin, the flesh, or the devil, preventing individuals from experiencing the freedom and abundant life offered through Jesus Christ. This concept is deeply rooted in the biblical narrative, illustrating the contrast between the bondage of sin and the liberty found in Christ.

A person could be enslaved spiritually and not even or not yet know it. The sinner first believes he is having fun. The chronically rebellious and disobedient have no idea that they are enslaved but instead think that they are living their own way by their own terms. Anything they are doing that is sinful, or ungodly is not natural in a man, nor is it inspired by God. So, there is only one other source of evil impulses. Yes, the devil. **We are not designed for sin, else we would not die after sinning and because of sin.**

The theme of spiritual slavery is mentioned in the Bible.

Truly, truly, I tell you, everyone who sins is a slave to sin. (John 8:34)

Sin is addictive. Sin is deadly; sin has bondage. A person could be on death row, just waiting. Perhaps this waiting is by the Grace of God to give that person a chance to get off of death row and out of bondage. When a man sins, his soul is fragmented into 7 parts immediately and each of those seven parts is put in separate prisons. This is deep bondage. Of course, when a person is imprisoned he is under the control of the warden or the guard. He is in bonds or bondage. A man may or may not know if he is spiritually captive and imprisoned. This depends on if he is spiritually attuned and paying attention or not. After some certain sin he may start to realize that his life is different. Things aren't as they used to be. Things don't work anymore as they used to; he feels he has fallen from favor. Maybe he has. Maybe he has fallen by that sin from Grace or is now under judgement of God, or even reproach has fallen on him. In this unrepented sinful condition he may be a candidate for spiritual slavery whether he realizes it or not. As said, he may be so distracted by all the fun he's having. He could be having this fun for years and decades before he notices that his life is really not working.

Do you not know that when you offer yourselves as obedient slaves, you are slaves to the one you obey, whether you are slaves to sin leading to death, or to obedience leading to righteousness? But thanks be to God that, though you once were slaves to sin, you wholeheartedly obeyed the form of teaching to which you were committed. You have been set free from sin and have become slaves to righteousness. (Romans 6:16-18)

To be in the bondage of sin or have freedom in Christ, that is our choice. Further, regarding spiritual slavery we read this verse:

Before this faith came, we were held in custody under the Law, locked up until faith should be revealed. So the Law became our guardian to lead us to Christ, that we might be justified by faith.(Galatians 3:23-24)

We can be forgiven of sins, delivered from bondage and spiritual prison and spiritual slavery if we are in Christ and we confess our sins and repent and ask for forgiveness of sins, transgressions, and iniquity. There is freedom from all this in Christ.

Yes, it is the bondage to sin and having to repeat it over and again such as ritual sex, for example. That might start out as exciting or enticing, but then it becomes drudgery.

For the good that I would I do not: but the evil which I would not, that I do.

Now if I do that I would not, it is no more I that do it, but sin that dwelleth in me.

I find then a law, that, when I would do good, evil is present with me.

For I delight in the law of God after the inward man:

But I see another law in my members, warring against the law of my mind, and bringing me into captivity to the law of sin which is in my members.

O wretched man that I am! who shall deliver me from the body of this death?
(Romans 7:19-25)

The law of sin is death. A person on death row is first imprisoned; he is captive. Now, will he sit there, or will he be enslaved and have to do some kind of work until his final punishment? The difference is captivity and sitting, or captivity and working. Deliverance is needed.

Why does anyone need deliverance? Because something spiritual has invaded or oppressed that person and they need a spiritual impact to be rid of it. When something that should not be there is there, a person may need deliverance. Deliverance can come through the Truth of God's Word--, simply hearing it. A person could be self-delivered or need the anointing and support and prayers of others. The one delivered must change, resist the devil and he will flee, but also remain in holiness and prayers and serving a Godly altar, else, how will the deliverance be maintained?

That impact may be prayer. It could be fasting. It could be raising an altar, which is always spiritual, and it could be <u>all</u> those things. Faithfully and diligently practicing all the disciplines of Christianity, which is the same as being all in. *All in* does mean having a pastor but not worshipping the pastor. Faithfulness and worship is to God and the Word of Truth.

When spiritually enslaved, you are driven to do things that you might not normally do. There is a power, a force, an anointing comes over you and it is evil. It drives you, worse than a crazy thirst, stronger than the worst craving, hankering, or urge. You must do a thing. The deception could be anywhere from feeling as if you do this, it will be the most satisfying and wonderful thing ever. Or, it could be that you feel that you **must** do it or *else*. I don't know what the *else* is. It could be that you feel that you will not be satisfied until you get or do this thing. It could be that you are so driven that you know that you will be tormented by some force or entity until you do it. This may have happened before, and you feel that you will not get any peace until you do it. And doing it means satisfying a demon, well--, for the time being, whether you realize that or not. Unless your soul is seared you will most likely feel guilt afterward. When the afterglow is not a glow but a raging hell fire then you really know you shouldn't have done that.

That is spiritual enslavement. That is no natural person coaxing or coercing you, but inside your own head or your own being is an impulse and impetus to do a thing that you actually know is not Godly, you know it is evil, but you may feel that you must do this thing.

You need deliverance. And you need a strong prayer life and to resist the devil so that he flees from you so he won't return after your full deliverance.

Enslaved

Were you a slave when you were called? Don't let it trouble you—although if you can gain your freedom, do so.(1 Corinthians 7:21)

Enslavement in the natural world is a sequela of spiritual enslavement, either right away or eventually. Worse than sin is the iniquity of sin and what it allows demons, devils, unclean spirits, and the like to do to a person. Sin is bad, but this part is worse. Sin could last a moment, whether it is pleasurable or not, but iniquity could last generations. Iniquity invites hell, no doubt.

For the good that I would I do not: but the evil which I would not, that I do.

Now if I do that I would not, it is no more I that do it, but sin that dwelleth in me.

I find then a law, that, when I would do good, evil is present with me. (Romans 7:19-21)

Don't be deceived, the devil is looking for the souls of men, to capture them, to buy them, to sell them, to trade them; to enslave them. (Revelation 18:13)

Slavery is harsh, but the definitions and examples have been outlined very well. But enslaving another person can be so subtle that it may not be detected for years, if ever. You, becoming enslaved may be so insipid that you may not know if it has happened to you, or when. This is especially true if it happens to you at a young age and you are "groomed" for it. It is especially true if it is done by a trusted someone such as a family member or other authority figure.

In the natural, do you seem to be:

- The one who works?
- The one who does all the work, while others don't do much or anything?
- The one whose pay is taken?
- The one who is disrespected?

- The one who should not complain, just be quiet and do for the rest?
- The one discriminated against?
- Stepped on like a steppingstone?
- Always helping others, but who will help you?
- Treated unfairly?

The devil will enslave for his own enrichment. The devil will enslave to thwart the plans of God. The devil will enslave to isolate a person who should not be isolated. To thwart destiny. To utterly wear a person down until he wears them out. The devil will use whoever he can to enslave another--, even a family member.

In the Old Testament, if a man sells his daughter as a servant, she is not to go free as male servants do. (Exodus 21:7). Explaining that, after 6 years of service the male servant can go free, it is called the year of Jubilee. However, if a man marries a woman or has a slave that he is not "pleased" with, she may go free without having to pay that man anything. However, shouldn't the question be, why would a man sell his child as a servant?

Evil? Would a man sell another man? Even his own child? The heart of man is evil, so the answer is yes.

In the old days a person might have given their child to the king because they loved the king so much. That male person might have to become a eunuch to serve the king. Becoming a eunuch means to become barren and also work as a slave. Have nothing, own nothing, not even have children. That is a whole other level of slavery. That is another form of sacrificing the child. People did that for their own advantage, back then.

I don't mean giving your child for priestly service as Hannah promised Samuel to God, but this was giving your child to another human in a high position, as a form of worship of that natural king or for advantage.

A eunuch was a servant, a slave so they were made barren financially. They were also eunuchs, so they were made barren reproductively as well. Those who sell their children are no different than those who sacrifice their children to Molech and Chemosh.

Desperation?

Is it the law? It's the law in the natural? It's the law in the spirit? In the natural, the man who died in debt had two sons who were about to be taken into servitude, but the widow woman pleaded with the Prophet of God to get enough to pay the debt.

It's the law in the spirit? Yes, it is the law of sin and death. The spiritual law is what makes all the other things that happen, happen. Unless, like Jesus, there is nothing in us that allows it. And that thing in a person that would allow this spiritual law to work against a man would be iniquity.

Jacob at Laban's ranch, did Laban not try to make him into a slave? Yes he did. Laban was his uncle and his father-in-law; a double relative and he was willing to steal from Jacob.

Witchcraft Enslavement

A curse causeless cannot alight.

Captured souls. The enemy doesn't just seek after and capture souls, the enemy is wicked. Through witchcraft, even body parts, organs, and extremities could be captured and enslaved. Know that enslaved doesn't mean sitting on a bench in a cell. Recall we've talked about forced labor of prisoners. Labor camps, forced labor, for use, or just for spite. The enemy of our souls could break folks down for parts. Even while alive, *parts* could be being used in strange places for strange things. It seems that the *part* is still there, it is just not serving the owner of that "part."

I've read a few books on deliverance of body parts, two of which were written by Stephen Beloved. In his first book https://a.co/d/7lrrIhU he outlines the deliverance of the head, legs, hands, tongue, and eyes. The second book: brain, womb, the blood, and ears. https://a.co/d/1kCpI4o The wickedness of the wicked is very wicked; even individual organs can be targeted, captured, and or enslaved.

The knowledge that *parts* can be separated is first amazing, and then very unsettling to frightening. Especially knowing that even *parts* of the soul can be broken away. Soul fragmenting is possible. Witches of a certain authority can steal, take, use, borrow, remove--, do all kinds of things to various body parts and organs of a person. I've heard various things said on deliverance grounds. For example, you wake up and your leg is tired or hurting or suddenly not working correctly, it may be said that a witch liked your leg or thought it would be fun to ride on your leg, using it as its vehicle, or as a table in a witch's coven all night. Do not take my word for any of this, pray and ask the Holy Spirit if it is true, if it is possible? Then ask Him how to pray to be protected against it. (Psalm 91 is an excellent before bedtime prayer.)

If you have a damaged organ or body part then pray for deliverance, healing, restoration or even renewal of that part. Don't be afraid to ask God to give you a new one. God made the first one, surely, He can make a new one. Amen.

Mostly we would think they can do this to other sinners. Yes. But a dry Christian can be susceptible to all kinds of evil spiritual manipulations. If you say you are in Christ, then **be all in**. Do not be dry, that is prayerless, and be sure to stay wet with the washing by the Water by the Word.

Prayer may not be automatic for all, although my stance is you pray what is in your heart. It is best to pray the Word of God if you don't even know where to start. Start in the Psalms, for example. And to become more diligent and knowledgeable in prayer, pray with others in person or online. Discipline requires doing. Prayer is a discipline of the faith.

If there is no iniquity in you, evil curses cannot alight. The purpose of the Law of God is to protect man from such. The Law of God is itself Holy. The man who keeps the law of God becomes also Holy. If there is no sin or iniquity in a man, a curse cannot alight on him. What saddens me for myself and anyone else is that a curse ever did or could alight on me, that means there was iniquity somewhere in me and I was not like Jesus. Of course, none of us are perfect, we all have sinned and fallen short of the Glory of God. That is why Jesus had to come and buy us back from the Curse of the Law which is sin, death, and poverty. I can boldly say that if you are experiencing any of those three things, you are still under the Curse of the Law, even if you profess Christ. Yes, being in Christ makes all things right—in the spirit, but it must also translate in the natural realm and that depends greatly on the believer, himself and it can take time.

For I was alive without the law once: but when the commandment came, sin revived, and I died. And the commandment, which *was ordained* to life, I found *to be* unto death. For sin, taking occasion by the commandment, deceived me, and by it slew *me.* Wherefore the law *is* holy, and the commandment holy, and just, and good. (Galatians 9-12)

Signs that You've Been Enslaved

The following are natural signs of spiritual slavery.

- When you lose and then someone else, or everyone else in the family, for example, wins.
- It seems the deck is stacked against you. Well, if this scenario keeps repeating, then it is. This is a pattern.
- Every time you are about to get something you don't.
- You may get something, but it gets taken away. For example, in bloodlines, no one has a car or keeps a car.

In certain bloodlines, does anyone have a house? In a family only one of the grown siblings owns a house. A fluke internal house flood wiped out half of that house, It had to be torn down to the rafters and rebuilt. In another bloodline the adult children owned houses but there was a total of four separate fires, over some years, and one wiped out one of the houses completely.

The one in that family who gets a house struggles and struggles and is under so much warfare, even from jealous brothers. Witches are covetous types who see a thing and want that thing, even if they have to take it from the person who owns it or has it.

It may not even be enemies who are trying to take or ruin the house, but he uses people against people. I was at a get together and a friend of the owner was present. There was casual eating, it was a Superbowl party. The guest in question, was a professional male, 40+ years old, dressed in a suit, for some reason, was seated on a very nice velvet couch with a small plate of hand food. He also had two napkins. Oh no, he didn't use the napkin; he wiped his fingers on the velvet cushions when he thought no one was looking. I'm always looking; the Lord has shown me so many things over the years that I wasn't even planning to see. These two had been "friends" for many years, yet this man was destroying his friend's property.

A different kind of witch wouldn't just destroy the property, they'd try to take it, or take something else, or punish the owner for having nice things or things that they covet, or better things than they do. I don't consider those who compete with me as friends. I don't make them into enemies either, but my eyes are open, and my prayer life is working.

More signs of spiritual slavery:

- Almost there (and they snatch you back)
- You work, work, work with little or nothing to show for it.
- You are exhausted and tired all the time, even in the morning when you wake up.
- You may get something but eventually it is gone. Either someone borrows it and never returns it, which

is stealing, or you have to use it for unforeseen emergencies.

- It just disappeared. Don't know where that went.
- When you get hurt, someone prospers in the family. There are curses and rituals set up that way.

Signs that a body part is enslaved:

- When things that used to work do not work anymore.

` Family most often means blood relatives, but family or household can mean anyone who has direct access to you, usually on a regular basis and knows your business, because you usually trust them and tell them your plans. Household or family also means people that you've let into your life, usually intimately by dating, sleeping with, or marrying them. It also includes ex's unless you have gotten a spiritual divorce from them in the Courts of Heaven.

Joseph's brothers literally made him a slave. People have often speculated why Jacob selected Ephraim and Manasseh, Joseph's twins for inheritance and not

Joseph—could it be because Joseph had been made a slave? Not by Jacob and not because he wasn't forgiven, but because the inheritances may have already been established before Jacob knew Joseph was still alive. Joseph was enslaved. He didn't partake of family blessings, he may have been taken care of elsewhere, but not given to by the hand of Jacob.

In order for Jesus to be Jesus, to be Savior, He had to have a known mother and father, unlike Melchizedek. The authority of a man had to be known in order for Jesus to come here and do the redemptive work that He did. Jesus was a descendant of Abraham and a Son of David, all fulfilling prophecy. Jesus was all man, as well, we know Jesus was all God. Jesus was never a slave, so there was no way inheritance would ever be blocked from Him. Joseph had no Redeemer because Jesus hadn't come yet.

Daniel had no redemption from slavery, although the Lord set him free, and he became a satrap in Babylon. Recall, Joseph rose to power in Egypt as well. Jesus had not come yet, so redemption was not possible for Daniel. The devil had nothing in Jesus and Jesus was never a slave.

Whereas most of the people groups in the entire world have been made into slaves at some time or other in history, it is only since the Resurrection of Jesus Christ and the Blood of the Better Covenant have we been able to be redeemed from the law of sin and death and therefore also freed from captivity and fully redeemed from slavery.

So, when it was discovered that Joseph was alive and he had the two twin boys, Joseph may have earned a double portion for his trouble. Joseph didn't need a blessing, but here are these two sons of his. Jacob said, These are my sons. By the time Joseph had these two boys he was no longer a slave, therefore Ephraim and Manasseh were never slaves. They received the inheritance.

In Christ, we are redeemed from sin and death, therefore we may receive inheritance. Ask for it. Accept it. Walk in it.

No one wants to be a slave, although I know a 12-year-old who used to brag that he was in Juvie because he was thuggish and wanted street cred. His father didn't stop him from saying that, and he is twice twelve now, and in prison this very day. Watch your mouth.

No matter how holy you are or think you are, you do not want to ever be accused of stealing a man and making him your slave. No. Not your own child and not a stranger who has come to you from bondage, do you bring him into bondage again. For this reason, you must treat those who work for you fairly. Do not hold them back and do not give them less than they are due. Those are devil tactics. Do not steal a man, no matter how desperate your situation seems. That also means that you respect your family; you don't enslave them.

Whoever steals a man and sells him, and anyone found in possession of him, shall be put to death. (Exodus 21:16)

If you feel that you have been enslaved by the enemy, and illegally so, take him to the Courts of Heaven and the Words says that if a man is stolen and sold, that thief must be put to death.

As far as being a support to your family and others, while God loves a cheerful and generous giver, I can love you, but I can't give myself away. I can love you, but I cannot risk destiny for your plans or carnal needs or desires. Some you must fulfill yourself.

Where Is Your Inheritance?

Reparations? People inherently know that something, or some things are missing. Generational wealth, yes, but current and individual wealth--, where is it? If you are still walking around in slave clothes, in the wrong garments... If you are still talking like a slave, walking like a slave, looking like a slave, thinking like a slave, etc...Then in the spirit you are still a slave.

So where is your inheritance? Has it bypassed you? Did your ancestors' inheritance bypass them and now it's your turn to receive it, but do you qualify?

Where is your stuff?

The Spirit of the Lord is on me, because he has anointed me to proclaim good news to the captives. Therefore, we must pray so that we receive our correct **inheritance** from our Father, as we are fully redeemed and *in Christ.*

Lord, let the spirit and the garment of the slave be totally removed from us, in the Name of Jesus.

God gave us all a garment, and it is **<u>not</u>** the garment of the slave. It is the garment of a son, a daughter. Nor has he given us the *spirit of a slave*. In Christ, we are sons and daughters of God.

Lord, restore to me my right garment, a clean and acceptable, even glorious garment, in the Name of Jesus.

Givers & Takers

Cinderella was a slave. A servant? Nope, a slave. Not only that, but the ones also who enslaved her were totally *anti-marriage*. Well, it was obvious that the two stepsisters were either not marriage material or nobody wanted them, but when they saw that their slave may have an opportunity for marriage and to a prince, no doubt, they were seriously anti-marriage. Still, it doesn't matter the motive, enslaving a person is still a crime in the spirit and even though on paper it should be in the natural, many times it seems to be looked over. For this reason, you need to handle your own freedom yourself and you do that *in Christ.*

Users and takers. Cinderella had everything going for her, so beside enslavement, her stepfamily wanted to cover her – in ashes, and work, and drudgery, and dirty clothes so she would not be attractive. Isn't that what slaves are made to be, do, and look like anyway? If your people group have ever been enslaved, then get in Christ and pray the spirit of the slave off of your bloodline. Pray that you get your right garments back. Do not let anyone force you to put on or keep on the garments of a slave. Do not keep on filthy garments.

Joseph **was** a slave, and there was a whole garment issue with Joseph, where the coat of many colors that his father gave him was taken from him and then he had to wear the garment of a slave.

Those natural acts do not just impact the natural, they impact the spirit realm. Folks come and go in the natural, but in the spirit, things live on and on, even for generations in bloodlines. That is, until someone stops it.

Slave owners and captors are notoriously pharaonic in behavior and they want to control that slave and keep them enslaved.

You're the strong one your family may tell you to your face. They may add, You can bear it. Save us!

Where giving and taking is taken through the extreme, there is slavery. Where one does all the work and the other or others receive all the benefits. Many countries have outlawed slavery on paper. The last country to formally abolish it was Mauritania in 1981, and it criminalized it only in 2007. However, modern slavery still affects an estimated 50+ million people worldwide, through forced labor, human trafficking, debt bondage, Child slavery, forced marriage, or domestic servitude.

You'd never put your child through any of this, would you?

There are countries where slavery is practiced openly or systematically, despite laws against slavery. Widespread slavery still exists in systemic form, either due to cultural practices, lack of enforcement, corruption, or state complicity:

In Mauritania, hereditary slavery still exists, especially among Afro-Mauritanians. The government has criminalized slavery, but prosecutions are rare. Slaves are often inherited through generations, particularly among the Haratin caste.

Since the fall of Gaddafi, Libya has become a hub for open-air slave markets. Migrants especially sub-Saharan Africans, are captured, sold, and exploited. Still.

Iran reports of forced marriage and child labor. Ethnic minorities such as Afghan migrants are subjected to forced labor, including in the military.

Sudan experiences abduction and enslavement of women and children during civil wars, especially by militias. Reports of human trafficking and sexual slavery persist.

Pakistan enforces debt bondage, and it is widespread in brick kilns and the agriculture industry. Whole families can be trapped for generations in unpaid labor.

India has the largest absolute number of modern slaves, approximately 8 million, per the Global Slavery Index. There is forced labor in construction, domestic work, and textiles. As well, there is sex trafficking. All the ways of a man are pure in his own eyes, therefore caste-based exploitation persists in rural areas.

In Bangladesh there is debt bondage, child labor, and forced prostitution is prevalent.

Afghanistan uses forced child labor, and sexual slavery called Baca Bazi where adolescent boys are toyed with by grown men. It is pedophilic and homophilic. The boys are usually poor or homeless. They are captured (my word) and forced to be humiliated and wear women's clothes and dance for grown men for their "entertainment," yet homosexuality is **criminal** in Afghanistan. In some cases, families facing extreme poverty or starvation may feel compelled to sell their young sons to a *bacha baz* or allow them to be "adopted" in exchange for food or money. Facing both social stigma and sexual abuse, the young boys, who often despise their captors, struggle with psychological effects from the abuse.

Forced marriages are also prevalent in this country.

Myanmar military uses forced labor, including child soldiers. Ethnic minorities, like the Rohingya, face exploitation and trafficking.

Nigeria has reports of human trafficking, forced labor, and ritual slavery. In other parts of West Africa there is a practice called *Trokosi* where virgin girls, some as young as six years old, are given to the shrine. Ghana, Togo, and Benin are known for this practice. The girl is given with or against her will in atonement for the sins of the family or in payment for services. Some families believe they are protecting their child by sending them to the shrine of the native and traditional priests. If the girl runs away or dies, then another from the family must take her place.

This is a never-ending cycle for those born into a family that would sacrifice them for their own protection, gain, or other reason. It is said that in some families they are on the third or fourth girl enslaved to the shrine and their daughter is considered to be married to the *god* or *gods* of that shrine. In the shrines they serve the priests, elders, or priests of these traditional religious shrines and are not paid anything.

In Africa, Boko Haram has enslaved women and children.

Democratic Republic of Congo uses child labor in mining, especially for cobalt. Armed groups use forced labor and sexual slavery.

Your Father's House

Thy father made our yoke grievous: now
therefore make thou the grievous service of
thy father, and his heavy yoke which he
put upon us, lighter, and we will serve
thee. (1 Kings 12:4)

Now we are going to make this more
personal than you may have thought. Slavery
in your father's house. Before you start
yelling that my father was not a slave, there's
no slavery in my family, keep reading.

If you are enslaved in the spirit, you
may be the slave of your family or some
other group. And the inverse is also true, if
you are the slave of your family, chances are
very good that you are enslaved in the spirit.

Scapegoat? Family scapegoat? Well,
at least a scapegoat was set free, eventually.

Well, it only was sent into the forest, which is another indication of captivity, but free, nonetheless. Still, it is the slave. How about the butler who gets blamed for everything that goes wrong? In this way a slave can be a scapegoat that is still tied and is not let go. This is far worse.

You may be expected to **be** the slave; you may have been groomed to be the slave. You may have auditioned or become an obedient slave, or entrapped as the slave. You went along with the program assigned to you and never bucked it.

In some cultures, the children are property of the parents, and the parents can use the children in any way they choose. They can select who and if they marry. The can collect a dowry, and the parents decide what that dowry is. They can decide that the child doesn't marry and that everything the child earns or gets they are fully entitled to it. All of it. The child's car, house, everything. Some think they can march into a company that their child owns and determine who can work there and who cannot, as if they have training and authority as CEO or owner. They think they can decide who can live in their child's house, because if the house is their child's, then it is also their house.

Culture *smulture*, this is slavery.

These overbearing pharaonic, slave-owner type parents also believe that they can take whatever one child has or owns and simply give it to another child in the family. As the child that is being ripped off, if you don't agree with the program, then the witchcraft really starts: control, domination, guilt-tripping, manipulation, intimidation. If you don't do as they say, you will be cut out of the family.

If you are, what will you miss?

This is not to say that witchcraft hadn't already started before the parents, or another sibling tried to make one child's property communal family property. But it steps up if the slave of the family is not compliant.

Slavery requires witchcraft to work, anyway; therefore, it is an offshoot of witchcraft, or witchcraft is an offshoot of slavery.

I cannot think of one "kingdom" on Earth that was not built on the backs of slaves. In the same way, whenever he can, the devil makes slaves of men to expand his kingdom of darkness. If you have been a slave master or come from a bloodline of slave masters, and have not found Christ and repented, you will have a day of reckoning, either on Earth or in the great beyond.

Repent.

And he said unto them, What counsel give ye that we may answer this people, who have spoken to me, saying, Make the yoke which thy father did put upon us lighter?

And the young men that were grown up with him spake unto him, saying Thus shalt thou speak unto this people that spake unto thee, saying, They father made our yoke heavy, but make though it lighter unto us; thus shalt thou say unto them, My little finger shall be thicker than my father's loins. And now whereas my father did lade you with a heavy yoke, I will add to your yoke: my father hath chastised you with whips, but I will chastise you with scorpions. (1 Kings 12:9-11, 1Kings 12:14)

At Work

If you are enslaved in the spirit you may be the one who works diligently but makes far less than the norm, or far less than everyone else who works at that same business in the natural.

Even if your boss is the mastermind of the operation and even if it is totally legit, the slave *belongs* to the master. Paid for? Well, if you agreed on a certain salary for a certain amount of work, isn't that a contract? So one might be *paid for.* When in that contract is that the work that a man does while he is employed there, that works belongs to the business if that discovery, invention, or other thing of value was made while the person worked for that company.

Over and again, we see inventions that slaves made in Colonial America that the slave master or other white man took credit for.

A man who was born and raised in Detroit, Michigan who had a God-idea to put a strip of rubber on the backs of cars to absorb the impact. He took the idea of all places to a car dealership; he didn't know what else to do or where else to take it. Next thing you know all cars have bumpers and he has nothing. Yes, people outrightly steal. Sometimes they size you up when they meet you and decide they can take you, or you're too nice or too passive and you won't do anything to them. So, they steal.

Then there are those that a person may work for who decide that every idea you have while you are working here belongs to me. If you sign an agreement to that, then it must stand, so be very careful what you willingly give away. Also stay prayed up in the Spirit so you God-ideas remain yours and benefit you.

Empaths & Narcissists

Some have warped ideas about relationships and marriages and may believe that their spouse is property and that a spouse should be a slave. It is sad to be a king and have one subject, just one: your spouse. That is a sad kingdom.

Some are born to pillage and attack others. Some are trained up that way. Some are sadists and love to inflict pain while others may be masochists who endure it because something in them makes them to endure it or not to uprise against it.

Many times, we see this dynamic in interpersonal relationships such as marriages. One evil spouse, one domestically abused spouse.

Know ye not, brethren, (for I speak to them that know the law,) how that the law hath dominion over a man as long as he liveth? For the woman which hath an husband is bound by the law to *her* husband so long as he liveth; but if the husband be dead, she is loosed from the law of *her* husband. So then if, while *her* husband liveth, she be married to another man, she shall be called an adulteress: but if her husband be dead, she is free from that law; so that she is no adulteress, though she be married to another man. (Galatians 3:1-3)

Tagged, Marked

A slave is tagged in the natural, His ear may be pierced, he is marked in some way, possibly branded.

These days, a prisoner or slave could be digitally tracked, like animals with embedded chips. Additionally, there are *spiritual* markings on a person or in their blood that indicate in the spirit who they are.

One such identification mark was the face mask. This could explain why people violently oppose wearing it because they know the historical significance of it. In the Transatlantic Slave Trade, especially in the Americas, iron face masks or muzzles were sometimes used on enslaved Africans—particularly women—as punishment or to prevent them from eating, speaking, or resisting. These were often called "scold's bridles" or "iron muzzles", and they could be cruel, sharp, and painful. The mask would sometimes have metal protrusions to prevent eating or cause discomfort when talking.

In Europe during the Middle Ages & Early Modern period, similar devices were used for punishing women accused of gossiping or insubordination—these were not exclusive to slaves, but also used on servants or prisoners.

In Ancient Rome or Greece, slaves were usually not masked, but they were branded, tattooed, or forced to wear collars with inscriptions identifying them as property.

The purpose of forcing slaves to wear masks was to dehumanize them. Masks made it easier to treat people as property. Silence them: Prevent talking, praying, or organizing. Feeding control: Prevent self-starvation or eating crops. And for

psychological control, to reinforce shame, fear, and submission.

Holy Ghost Fire surround me so I cannot be tracked, in the Name of Jesus.

Lord, track those who are tracking me, in the Name of Jesus.

Lord, by the Blood of Jesus blot out every mark on me and in me that identifies me as a slave, in the Name of Jesus.

Monitoring and familiar spirits tracking me, receive Fire of the Holy Ghost and fall down and die, in the Name of Jesus.

There was a man in the Old Testament who died in debt. That debt not only marked him, it marked his two sons. Their mother was in great distress and called on the prophet of God. Elisha asked her what she had in the house. She said she had nothing but a jar of oil. Elisha told her to gather empty vessels, and the oil miraculously multiplied until every jar was filled. She sold the oil, paid off her debt, and lived on the rest. Clear case of financial need met by a prophet through a miracle. On the front end of that story, it was a clear case of the deceased father having to borrow and get into debt with creditors and either not solving the problem of debt, or not being able to solve it. It is a clear case of a man who didn't clear his debt, be it spiritual, financial, natural or all of those kinds of debt and leaving the problem to his children. Now his children would be enslaved to pay for the father's debt.

Parents can enslave their children by taking over their lives and their careers and bank accounts. Parents can enslave their children by leaving them spiritual and or natural debt.

Doesn't an animal try to mark territory? How much cleaning do you have to do to keep a puppy from using a spot when he smells urine? If a person is marked, it draws more of the same to what it is marked with.

You shall not give up to his master a slave who has escaped from his master to you. He shall dwell with you, in your midst, in the place that he shall choose within one of your towns, wherever it suits him. You shall not wrong him. (Deuteronomy 23:15-16 ESV)

Sadly here, once victimized, raped, pillaged a person can receive a mark such as the *spirit of victim* or the *spirit of rape* and that makes them susceptible to the same thing happening to them again, unless deliverance is had.

In the natural, this seems to be what happens by or because of a person enduring a thing and saying nothing about it or against it. In the natural, people think they are okay with that. They think it is okay to ask their brother for their last dollar and out of love her big brother shares all he has while the little sister uses the money to go shopping or go to a restaurant with her friends. Big brother is suffering, but he has gone along with what was asked, thinking it was a need, when it was only a want; now he is suffering silently. Don't we think to suffer silently is Christian behavior? Is her brother volunteering for slavery?

Well, is it? What message does it send to others in the natural? What message does it send in the spirit realm? Even if you say nothing in the natural, this must be handled in the spirit realm. Jesus opened not His mouth when He was scourged and beaten, but was He not praying?

Saints of God then I will warn you that even when you go through something spiritual that you know the devil orchestrated, but the Lord brings you through, Hallelujah! But, be sure to **condemn** the devil's plot, plan, and scheme and declare that it shall not happen to you again. Else, a door is opened, and that open door may say it's okay to do this again.

Sealed

Once sealed into slavery, the slave master can do many things, if not anything to the slave.

After Lazarus had already been dead for days, Jesus arrived on the scene and said, Roll away the stone. The stone had sealed the tomb. Jesus required them to roll away the seal and then let Lazarus come out and be alive and free again. In the same way, the seal of slavery must be removed from you so you also can be alive and free again.

Not only that, the stone also had to be rolled away from the tomb that Jesus was lain in. the stone is a stone of the iniquity of sin. Sin is the breaking of spiritual law and it leads to death. Once sentenced a person is imprisoned wither spiritually or in the natural, or both and the case is "sealed." The stone is a natural mark that a seal has been placed.

Here comes Jesus once again, confounding the wise; He has become the chief cornerstone. He is the thing they tried to kill Him with, so it would have been impossible. Jesus is the Capstone as well. What stone would ever betray Jesus?

> I will also give him a white stone with a new name written on it, known only to him who receives it. (Revelation 2:17)

Sex Slave

For the sexually immoral, for those practicing homosexuality, for slave traders and liars and perjurers—and for whatever else is contrary to the sound doctrine, (1 Timothy 1:10)

In the natural there are more than 50 million slaves worldwide. It is estimated that approximately that at least 10 percent of those are sex slaves. Slavery is still legal in a number of countries.

While slavery is officially illegal in every country in the world, the reality is more complicated. Modern forms of slavery still exist in nearly every region, and in some countries, slavery-like practices are tolerated, ignored, or even functionally legal through lack of enforcement or cultural tradition.

There are countries with widespread human trafficking or modern slavery (though less systemic) These countries may not have state-sanctioned slavery, but are major sources or destinations for trafficked and exploited people. China has forced labor in Xinjiang (Uyghur Muslims), trafficking, and state oppression.

Russia – Migrant exploitation, human trafficking.

Qatar & Gulf States – Kafala system traps migrant workers in abusive labor conditions.

North Korea – State-run forced labor camps, some of the most extreme in the world.

United Arab Emirates – Domestic workers and migrants face conditions bordering on slavery.

Thailand – Human trafficking in fishing and sex industries.

United States – Migrant labor exploitation, sex trafficking, prison labor which is legal under 13th Amendment exception.

Modern slavery is not about ownership like in the past. Today, it's about control, coercion, and exploitation — and it exists in every country, including developed ones. How many stories have we heard even in the USA where a person comes to work for a rich family, but they get trapped in abusive labor conditions. For example, the family doesn't let their maid leave the house. Some have been locked in their rooms. They work without pay. Room and board? Yes, but no pay and they can't leave? That is incarceration; it is slavery.

Even within families a person could get trafficked.

You're the pretty one, go out here and make some money for this family. A man tells his sister that she is so pretty she should be a model, and he knows a guy who is a photographer who can help her build a portfolio. She doesn't bite. Next, this same guy is shooting for a clothing line, and she can make some money. She says, really? She goes to the shoot, and it progresses from a clothing shoot to a pantyhose shoot to the "photographer" wanting her to basically take her top off. She gets out of there. Did that man sell his sister out or try to? God knows, but if he did, he was trying to exploit her into some version of the sex trade. If he was ignorant of the photographer's intent, then he was ignorant and he would still be judged because a man's role is to protect women, not exploit them.

There are too many stories of refugees or people seeking asylum and entering the USA for example, at the Southern Border where human coyotes are treacherously situated along the way. They may ask a family for their child (female or male, for the night, longer, or permanently) in exchange for helping them reach the border.

No one is to be made into a slave according to the Word of God. Woe to those who do that, especially to brothers and sisters in the faith. Woe to wolves who come into the House of God looking for victims. And there is judgment for opportunists who are in the faith yet still targeting others also in the faith.

> If any of your fellow Israelites become poor
> and sell themselves to you, do not make
> them work as slaves. (Leviticus 25:39)

SRA

The spirit world will make or try to make a human into a sex slave. SRA … The victims of this are tormented at staggering levels. This first became a thing to be talked about in the 1970's and 1980's but carnal minded people explained it away as hallucination, dreams, such as nightmares, or made-up memories.

These are spiritual things that are happening to people. While it is pure torment to the individual, the only thing worse than it happening is not knowing that it is happening. Not understanding what it is. Not having a way to express it to anyone. Not having anyone who will believe you. Falsely blaming someone in the natural, especially when there are physical signs when you wake up in the morning, for example. Serial ritual abuse is spiritual slavery. And the worst of all is not having anyone to help you get free.

Spirit spouse is a serial, spiritual sex offender and rapist. Male or female it doesn't matter, the victim is basically made into a sex slave until they make it stop. Get deliverance if you are having sex in the dream; that is a demon, no matter who it looks like or has disguised itself to look like.

In the spirit a person could be a whole spiritual prostitute and not even know it.

Deep deliverance is needed sooner than later. While anyone is waiting on deliverance, begin by getting saved. Then renounce and denounce the sins that put you in the predicament that you may find yourself, then begin full repentance both for yourself and down your bloodline. Your ancestors may be the reason you are suffering, and it may not even be anything you have done.

The Witchcraft of Favoritism

In the natural, in a family for example we may see favoritism. Favoritism on any team or in the workplace will create huge problems. Favoritism in the family, the same.

Favoritism in the workplace--, anywhere really, but especially at work is witchcraft. Not only that it can lead to more witchcraft.

Many of the world's richest countries and most beautiful ancient cities were built with slave labor. Many have been saved by the slaves they forced labor from. Joseph, for instance. Had he not been in Egypt, would they have survived the famine? It was because God was preserving Israel, and the Tribes of Israel and Joseph had been sold there that Egypt enjoyed the benefits of

Joseph's dreams, interpretations and stewardship so there was provision for Egypt and other peoples during that massive famine. However, many of the poorest today still carry economic or social scars from that system. Understanding this isn't about guilt — it's about clarity and truth.

Many of the world's richest people or most affluent families were built by slavery. Favoritism in a family means that the one or ones not favored are the slaves.

Two sisters cooked and set everything in place for the out of state wealthy aunts who were coming to visit their mother. When the two aunts arrived, they just about looked through the two sisters who were greeting and ready to feed them to ask for the other two sisters who were not present and had not done any work, but obviously were the two favorite sisters of their mother, the sister to these two affluent, fancy, city aunts.

Favor is not fair. No it is not, but it can be painful for the one who is not favored who either has or felt that they have met all the conditions of at least being accepted in the family.

In Genesis, Joseph who was righteous was sold into slavery and worked as a slave. His own brothers did that – that is a case of Hebrews enslaving other Hebrews, (Genesis 37:28). Families enslave their own family members, but in the case of Joseph they sold him not so much for gain but for spite.

But certain kinds of families knowingly or unknowingly will often choose a family member who supports the family, takes care of the family, while getting the short end of the stick while doing the most for the entire family. That slave is usually willing, thinking this is how family is, this is how family does. They may not find out until later that no one was planning to pay him or her back, not even in kindness, much less hard cash for monies, "lent" or given.

Then there are favorites in the family – the slave is **not** the favorite.

The slave of the family is not hated either, as long as they are giving the family

93

what they want. Maybe the family is in a certain condition of desperation, and they know they need to lean on someone, it should be God, but instead they may choose the *oldest* in the family to go out and work to help support the family. But it doesn't always have to be the oldest.

They may tell the talented one: go out and make some money for this family. They may tell (spoken or unspoken) expect the pretty one to make some money for this family. They may tell the strong one, or the smart one to go out and earn money for the family. Is this not enslavement? Then they resent that breadwinner when they want to use their own money their own way. or they meet someone and want to get married and live their own life and they may harass the in-law because they want the family dynamic to stay the same; they want the child's money and earning potential to stay for the benefit of the family of origin. (And you may have wondered why your in-laws don't like you.) You may have married the only successful one in the family, and they want his money to stay with them. They may feel that you are messing with the money system of the family. Unless you have more than they do and they expect you to give them money. Give them a gift or two and see if things change.

The slave is not bold enough to stand up to this. Will they ever leave and cleave to their new spouse and family. Is that person not a slave? Stuck in the family dynamics of their childhood?

Later, that benevolent *provider* may still not have anything because they gave it all away to their "family" who simply used it up. Many times, the users have their own money, but they want more so they ask the person in the family who they think has more or has enough to share. Sometimes, they ask the person who they think has too much because they think in a family everyone should earn and have the same.

This may smack of their childhoods when their parents told them to share so each could have an equal amount. That does not translate into adulthood.

There was a man who earned a very good living whose mother was a pastor. Her church was out of state, but he said he didn't tithe to support her ministry because if he did she would count his money and ask for more. That man had decided not to be a slave in the family.

But the *slave* may think: If I buy them a car or a house, or one more thing, then they won't be jealous of what I have.

If you buy yourself a Rolls Royce and buy your family member a brand-new Chevy, they may still not appreciate you. How dare you have a Rolls Royce? Without realizing it, they may be thinking, how can our slave have such a nice car?--, inferring that they are wasting money. Didn't Judas begrudge Jesus for being anointed with the precious ointment from the alabaster box saying we could have sold it and given to the poor?

That is proved out when Judas SOLD Jesus for the price of a slave, 30 pieces of silver. A slave shouldn't have nice things. A slave shouldn't have anything. A slave should work and earn but not have or enjoy. This could all be subconscious in the mind of anyone around anyone at any time.

While the slave may be thinking, If I do this, that, or the other, they will love me.

Love is a gift given it is not gotten by works—real love. There is another kind that you can buy.

Ephesians 2:8-9 8 For by grace are ye saved through faith; and that not of yourselves: it is the gift of God: 9 Not of works, lest any man should boast.

Favoritism leads to witchcraft and evil anyway. Joseph WAS the favorite and so the evil brothers got rid of Joseph by control and manipulation, and lies. Joseph was a slave in Egypt. It is the slave who works the hardest or the most diligently for the family. It is the slave who takes care of them even when they have little or nothing or say they have little or nothing, or not enough.

In Genesis 41:53-47:12 we read that there was a famine in Israel and the years of plenty in Egypt had come to an end. Therefore, there was a famine over all the land.

Jacob sent his sons to Egypt because Egypt had grain. There Joseph is the one who saved the family alive. In this case it doesn't mean that the older brothers didn't work as to why they didn't have enough, but it shows how the enslaved one benefits the others so much.

Online, I came across so many stories that you may say are made up, fiction or how people were mistreated in their families when they were the ones blessing the families. That is not an untrue human plight. The reason those stories are popular is because they are possible and people identify with them, even on some level. Most of them are based on favoritism of one while the other is dissed. Seeing a few of these stories, I asked the Lord why are these stories popular?

Because it is the human condition, even now. People identify with many of those stories because it, or something like it happened to them, whether they ever told anyone or not. They may have never admitted how much it hurt them to anyone. Maybe they simply internalized it. Now, how the problem is handled is another story and we are in Christ we don't do as the world does.

So, Joseph – was a slave and then demoted from slavery to prisoner, then promoted because of his spiritual gifting to dream interpreter to pharaoh then promoted to prime minister.

(See my books, **The Robe, Book 1,** **https://a.co/d/3M79siY** and **The Robe, Book 2: The Lessons of Joseph** https://a.co/d/1wabh63 which cover much more on what Joseph went through.)

Purpose of the Yoke

Of course, no one should ever want to be jailed or incarcerated. Incarceration is the highest form of slavery in the natural.

All who are under the yoke of slavery should consider their masters worthy of full respect, so that God's name and our teaching may not be slandered. (1 Timothy 6:1)

Chain gangs, prisoners tied together are not just a thing of the past, they still exist. The purpose of the yoke is to get work out of an animal in a controlled way, usually tied together by the yoke, to other animals. Collective captivity.

Careful. Without even realizing it, and not even being related by blood, you can tie yourself to a person under judgment by

God. If God is restraining a person for example, by cutting off their finances, but you decide to step in and give them money, you have just joined in their judgment. Always ask GOD if you should give, lend, or "help" so you don't interfere with anything He is doing. In putting your money in, you have yoked yourself to this person in an ungodly alliance.

In Medieval times, the yoke, as in a stockade, was a punishment. Would you willingly walk up to a person in a stockade and ask to join them in their humiliation? Do not ever think yourself wiser than God.

Prisoners tied or yoked together are called chain gangs, and they still exist, though they're rare and highly controversial. Those prisoners, in a sense, are yoked together. Chain gangs are groups of prisoners chained together at the ankles (or wrists) while performing forced manual labor, typically in public, building roads, picking up trash, or clearing brush. They were most common in the U.S. South from the late 19th to mid-20th centuries, often as a brutal extension of post-slavery racial control. Eddie Murphy, Martin Lawrence and Bernie Mac made and released a funny movie about it called, *Life in 1999*. But there is nothing funny about really being in a chain gang.

Chaining people together is another way of yoking them, as one might farm animals. In the USA, allegedly chain gangs were abolished in most states by the 1950's up to the 1970's due to human rights concerns and public backlash.

The practice of chain gangs was briefly revived in the 1990s during the "tough on crime" era. In Alabama (1995) it was reintroduced there for a time.

Arizona (Maricopa County) under Sheriff Joe Arpaio used chain gangs, including female and juvenile inmates. This drew heavy criticism.

Today, very few prisons still use chain gangs in public. But that doesn't mean that prisoners are not forced into doing labor and labor for little or no pay. Which still makes them slaves.

Give her of the fruit of her hands; and let her own works praise her in the gates.
(Proverbs 31:31)

God says that people, even women should be paid for their work. However, when in captivity, a person is just in captivity. The judgments of God were often that the habitual sinner would go into captivity. The devil abuses this for individuals whenever he can.

Chain gangs mostly stopped being a thing due to human rights concerns. They were widely considered cruel, degrading, and dehumanizing. Lawsuits and public pressure and civil liberties groups challenged their legality.

For safety reasons a person cannot even be shackled while on a plane. Even if transporting a dangerous prisoner.

Prison labor is common today. Inmates in most U.S. states still perform forced labor which is legal under the 13th Amendment exception for prisoners) Some make furniture or license plates. They farm, do laundry, and maintenance. In California they fight wildfires.

If there is any pay, it is often as low as a few cents an hour, or nothing at all.

Prisoners may work in crews, but they have no chains. They still have one or more guards over them, usually with weapons. Some prisoners still do roadside cleanup, landscaping, or disaster relief, but usually without shackles or chains. When road work, for example, is done under work-release programs or as part of rehabilitation, there is usually not a weaponized guard in their midst.

Outside the U.S., the chain gang is rare, but forced prison labor does still occur in countries such as China, North Korea, Russia, and some Gulf states. China has labor prison camps where even political dissidents are imprisoned. Russia has penal colonies with hard labor. North Korea has gulags with extreme forced labor.

Get out of spiritual enslavement before things translate to the natural.

Therefore shalt thou serve thine enemies which the LORD shall send against thee, in hunger, and in thirst, and in nakedness, and in want of all things: and he shall put a yoke of iron upon thy neck, until he have destroyed thee. (Deuteronomy 28:48)

(Break free from Collective Captivity, by this author: https://a.co/d/i0HNJCS)

In Christ

How can a person get out of slavery? How can a person buy their freedom? How can they pay a price that seems impossible to pay?

In God all things are possible.

The U.S. Constitution's 13th Amendment abolished slavery except as punishment for a crime, which is how forced prison labor remains legal. It is often described as "modern-day slavery" by critics.

In Christ, we are made free by Christ's redemptive work at Calvary. Even though we are nearly at the back of this book, first we must be saved and in Christ--, all the way in, not just playing around the edge.

Then we have to know who we are in Christ and know that we are free.

Freedom in Christ: The antidote to spiritual slavery is found in the person and work of Jesus Christ which offers the believer power over sin, death, and iniquity, bringing us to freedom in Him.

It is for freedom that Christ has set us free. Stand firm, then, and do not be encumbered once more by a yoke of slavery. (Galatians 5:1)

Iniquity is the residual of sin and death and even after a person is saved they still could have leftover debt to pay. Sometimes until you enforce your freedom on a demon that has come to punish and oppress, you may not have it. That demon may claim the right because of iniquity, yours, or from an ancestor in your bloodline.

Therefore, there is now no condemnation for those who are in Christ Jesus. For in Christ Jesus, the law of the Spirit of life set you free from the law of sin and death. (Romans 8:1-2)

Prince of the *Rematch*

Not only that, the devil will keep approaching even a saved person and keep trying to tempt them and entrap them into sin, bondage, yokes, and iniquity all over again. The devil may be the *prince of the rematch*. Satan must have been the one who started the idea of the **rematch because God doesn't lose battles. It is the loser who always wants the rematch**.

The devil either doesn't understand, *No*. Or, he pretends not to understand it. The passage in the Wilderness Temptations even say that he left Jesus, for a time.

He understands defeat in God, but when it comes to man he will resurface or try to do so, unless he is rebuked by God or totally destroyed. Temptations and deceptions are presented often, sometimes daily to try to re-enslave a Christian who has already been set free.

A spiritual yoke can be symbolic of one who is yoked to sin, to the bondage of sin. In addition, it can be a yoke that ties a person together with other like people, such as other sinners. That can be especially prevalent in a family, as in collective captivity. However, you won't get away from the spiritual issues by just being physically away from your kinfolks. By hating them or shunning them--, nope that won't do it. You must do the spiritual work yourself to be in Christ, all the way in and be set free from ancestral and bloodline iniquities and enslavement.

Remember, even saved folk can still be in sin, bondage, and even yokes.

Now therefore why tempt ye God, to
put a **yoke** upon the neck of
the disciples, which neither our fathers nor
we were able to bear? (Acts 15:10)

Hating them, getting angry at them, cussing folk out--, none of that will release you from bloodline iniquity. If you were the one enslaved do not, like the unsaved do, seek revenge. Vengeance belongs to God and that doesn't mean that we won't get to see it, because the Word says that we will get to see the downfall of our enemies. However, to get out of slavery and after getting out of slavery and in order to stay out of slavery, it is not done by revenge.

Only with thine eyes wilt thou behold and see the reward of the wicked. (Psalm 91:

Stand fast therefore in
the liberty wherewith Christ hath
made us free, and be not entangled again w
ith the **yoke** of bondage. (Galatians 5:1)

Breaking Free

First of all, find out if you are captive or enslaved. Captivity is one thing, it is imprisonment, spiritual or otherwise. Slavery is another thing, it is having to work for free with little or no freedoms.

So, you know or believe you are a slave. Now you have to find out who you are enslaved to. Then you need to find out why. Is this a judgment of God? Then your prayer will be different than if you are battling a demon combatant. But either way start with repentance and ask for God's Mercy. There should be deep repentance and deep cries for Mercy if you are under judgment from God because no one and no other thing can help you.

Father, is that You? Have I been turned over to reprobate? Have you taken Your hands off me? Lord, turn your face back to me, in the Name of Jesus.

If God does not have you under judgment, Hallelujah; there is hope for you. Know that you know that you are saved. Repent for the sin that caused the captivity and the enslavement. Denounce the sin, whether you did it or someone in your ancestral bloodline. Then ask for the Holy Spirit of God. Ask the Holy Spirit to help you. Be covered by the Blood of Jesus. Now you go into spiritual warfare if you are battling an enemy that has enslaved you. You need to get out of captivity. If you need to go into the Courts of Heaven, then do that.

Lord, BREAK every satanic seal over my life, in the Name of Jesus.

People dedicated their children to kings back in the day, nowadays that means dedication to evil entities in the spirit.

LORD, break every evil dedication of my life, break every evil dedication of the work of my hands and the fruit of my labor.

Break every evil dedication off of my destiny, and gifts, and skills, talents, and abilities, in the Name of Jesus.

I am not a slave. I am not a slave. In Christ Jesus, I am not a slave.

- I am not a barren slave.
- I am not barren; I am fruitful
- I am not a eunuch.
- I am not a slave.
- I am not your slave.
- I am not a slave to the enemy of God.
- I am a bondservant of Christ.
- And in Christ, I am free.

The Spirit of the Lord is on me, because he has anointed me to proclaim good news to the poor. He has sent me to proclaim freedom for the prisoners and recovery of sight for the blind, to set the oppressed free, (Isaiah 6:1, Luke 4:18)

Slave clothes- I tear you off. I take off captivity, in the Name of Jesus.

I put off slave clothes, collar, manacle, shackle, every chain on the captive. I take captivity captive, in Chris, in the Name of Jesus.

Every interference with my work, pay, salary, or promotions currently, or retroactively, fall down and die, in the Name of Jesus.

Every interference with my education, certificates, or diplomas or other credentials, I dismantle and remove that interference, in the Name of Jesus.

Gates of my profession, career, education, marriage, children, LIFT UP and be ye ever lift up, you everlasting doors, the King of Glory is coming in and I am in Christ. Amen.

Every illegal spiritual alien trying to enter or re-enter at the GATES of my life, I raise an altar against you, in the Name of Jesus.

Every diversion of anything that God gave me, sent me, prepared for me to have, Thief, Emptier, Waster, Devourer, Destroyer, captor, former captor, slave master, former slave master, abusive domestic person, every evil human agent, let it go, let it go right now, in the Name of Jesus.

Every lost thing, every lost coin, dollar, dime, or penny, find me now, find me now, in the Name of Jesus.

Any suffering, any slavery, any debts, spiritual or physical, natural that I can't repay, Blood of Jesus, pay for me, in the Name of Jesus. (x2 or more)

Any evil relative, any ignorant relative, any rebellious relative, any jealous relative, cease and desist or incur the wrath of God, in the Name of Jesus. I am God's property. Amen.

Every pharaonic priest, every pharaonic spirit trying to hold me in slavery, be drowned forever in the Red Sea, in the Blood of Jesus, in the Name of Jesus.

On Mount Zion, there shall be holiness, holiness, holiness, I am no longer bound by sin, in the Name of Jesus.

There is no smell of smoke on me from bondages, yokes or sin, in the Name of Jesus.

Territorial gates – Gates of where I live, open up, lift up, the King of Glory is coming in, the Lord, strong and mighty in battle, lift up and be ye ever lift up, in the Name of Jesus.

Educational gates – open up to me and be ye lift up, the King of Glory is coming in and I am in Christ.

Professional Gates – Gates of my chosen profession, open to me, in the Name of Jesus.

Evil human agents, household witch's, altars burn, burn, to ashes.by Holy Ghost Fire, Fire, Fire, in the Name of Jesus.

Any part of me working for any evil one, any evil thing, any evil power or entity in the spirit or natural, I cease to work for you, right now. I cease to be taken advantage of, right now. I cease to be your slave. The Blood of Jesus buys me out of every slave contract ever placed on my head or in my bloodline, in the Name of Jesus. Amen.

I break the power and sequelae of any ritual done on me, especially money ritual, by the power in the Blood of Jesus, in the Name of Jesus. (X7)

I send Fire to anyone who has ever done money ritual on me, in the Name of Jesus.

I break every evil exchange of virtues, gifts, talents, skills, destiny, wealth, health, aging or beauty done on me, in the Name of Jesus, I reverse the exchange by the power in the Blood of God's Christ.

Lord, let the fruit of my labor, yes money is a fruit, and also my joy and my peace in your work in the working of my hands, let that fruit come to me and may I never be denied it again, in the Name of Jesus.

Father, when the trees of the field yield their fruit and the Earth yields it's increase and I am safe in the land, then I will know that You Are the Lord, in the Name of Jesus. (Ezekiel 34:27, ESV)

Father, when you break the bands of my yokes and deliver me from the hand of those that have enslaved me, then I shall know that You are the Lord. (Ezekiel 34:27 ESV)

LORD, bring me out from under the
burdens of the Egyptians and deliver me
from slavery to them. Redeem me, LORD,
with an outstretched arm and with great
acts of judgement, in the Name of Jesus
(Exodus 6:6 ESV)

Because of slavery, Lord, I cry out for help.
Let my cries of rescue from slavery come up
to You, Lord God. (Exodus 2:23)

Lord, I shall remember the day, I came
out from Egypt, out of the
house of **bondage**; by strength of the
hand the LORD. (Exodus 13:3)

Lord, bring me out of the house of bondage,
in the Name of Jesus.

That the LORD sent a prophet unto the
children of Israel, which said unto
them, Thus saith the LORD God of
Israel, I brought you up from Egypt, and
brought you forth out of the
house of **bondage**; (Judges 6:8)

It is for freedom that Christ has set us free.
Stand firm, then, and do not let yourselves
be burdened again by a yoke of slavery.
(Galatians 5:1)

You are the LORD God, bring me out of all
bondage, yokes, and slavery as you did the
Hebrews out of Egypt, in the Name of Jesus.
(Galatians 4:3)

You are the LORD, break me out of the bands of every yoke that I may go upright, in the Name of Jesus. (Leviticus 26:13)

You shall remember that you were a slave in the land of Egypt, and the Lord your God brought you out from there with a mighty hand and an outstretched arm. Therefore the Lord your God commanded you to keep the Sabbath day. (Deuteronomy 5:15)

You are the Lord, my God who brought me out of the land of Egypt and out of the house of slavery. (Deuteronomy 5:6)

I am the Lord your God, who brought you out of the land of Egypt, that you should not be their slaves. And I have broken the bars of your yoke and made you walk erect. (Leviticus 26:13)

For thou hast broken the **yoke** of his burden, and the staff of his shoulder, the rod of his oppressor, as in the day of Midian. (Isaiah 9:4)

And it shall come to pass in that day, *that* his burden shall be taken away from off thy shoulder, and his **yoke** from off thy neck, and the **yoke** shall be destroyed because of the anointing. (Isaiah 10:27)

Is not this the fast that I have chosen? to loose the bands of wickedness, to undo the heavy burdens, and to let the oppressed go free, and that ye break every **yoke**? (Isaiah 58:6)

Lord, break the **yoke** of the king of Babylon. (Jeremiah 28:4) (X3)

Then Hananiah the prophet took the **yoke** from off the prophet Jeremiah's neck, and brake it. (Jeremiah 28:10)

Lord, take the yoke off my jaws, in the Name of Jesus. (Hosea 11:4)

Lord, break the enemy's yoke off of me and burst my bond into pieces, in the Name of Jesus. (Nahum 1:13)

Free me Loose me, Lord, Unchain me

Untie me. Unlock me, Lord, in the Name of Jesus.

I am free by the power in the Blood of Jesus, and by His Covenant of Grace with us.

I am free by the Spirit of the Living God, in the Name of Jesus.

Lord, let me come out of slavery with many spoils, having spoiled the Egyptians that enslaved me, all these many days, all these weeks, all these months, or all these years, in the Name of Jesus.

And the LORD gave the people favour in the sight of the Egyptians, so that they lent unto them *such things as they required*. And they spoiled the Egyptians. (Exodus 12:36)

Lord, let me come out of slavery with many spoils, having spoiled the Egyptians that enslaved me, all these many days, all these weeks, all these months, or all these years, in the Name of Jesus.

LORD, You are lowly and meek; let me take Your yoke upon myself and learn of You to find rest for my soul, in the Name of Jesus. (Matthew 11:29)

I seal these words, declarations across every realm, dimension, age, timeline, past, present and future to infinity . I seal them with the Blood of Jesus and the Holy Spirit of Promise.

Any retaliation against any person reading, speaking, hearing or praying these words and prayers, backfire against the perpetrator to infinity, without Mercy, in the Name of Jesus.

AMEN.

Dear Reader:

Thank you for acquiring and reading this book. I pray it has been an eye-opener and will facilitate your deliverance and full freedom.

In Jesus' Name,

Amen.

Dr. Marlene Miles

Prayerbooks by this author

While most books by this author have prayer points either throughout the book or at the end, there are some books that are only prayers. You just open up the book and pray.

Prayers Against Barrenness: *For Success in Business and Life*

Fruit of the Womb: *Prayers Against Barrenness*

Beauty Curses, *Warfare Prayers Against* https://a.co/d/5Xlc20M

Courts of Marriage: Prayers for Marriage in the Courts of Heaven *(prayerbook)* https://a.co/d/cNAdgAq

Courtroom Warfare @ Midnight *(prayerbook)* https://a.co/d/5fc7Qdp

Demonic Cobwebs *(prayerbook)*
https://a.co/d/fp9Oa2H

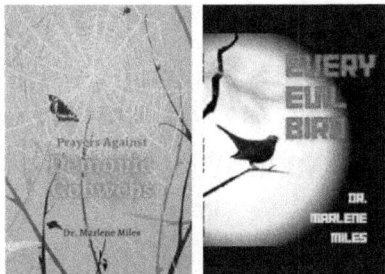

Every Evil Bird https://a.co/d/hF1kh1O

Gates of Thanksgiving

Spirits of Death, Hell & the Grave, Pass Over Me and My House

Throne of Grace: Courtroom Prayer

Warfare Prayer Against Poverty
https://a.co/d/bZ611Yu

Other books by this author

AK: The Adventures of the Agape Kid

Already Married in the Spirit: *Why You May Not Be Married in the Natural*

AMONG SOME THIEVES
https://a.co/d/dkYT4ZV

Ancestral Powers

Anti-Marriage, *The Spirit of*

Backstabbers https://a.co/d/gi8iBxf

Barrenness, *Prayers Against*
https://a.co/d/feUltIs

Battlefield of Marriage, *The*

Beware of the Dog: Prayers Against Dogs in the Dream.

Bless Your Food: *Let the Dining Table be Undefiled*

Blindsided: *Has the Old Man Bewitched You?* https://a.co/d/5O2fLLR

Break Free from Collective Captivity

Broken Spirits & Dry Bones

By Means of a Whorish Father

Casting Down Imaginations

Churchzilla, The Wanna-Be, Supposed-to-be Bride of Christ

Demonic Cobwebs (prayerbook)

Demonic Time Bombs

Demons Hate Questions

Devil Loves Trauma, *The*

Devil Weapons: Unforgiveness, Bitterness,...

The Devourers: Thieves of Darkness 2

Do Not Swear by the Moon

Don't Refuse Me, Lord (4 book series) https://a.co/d/idP34LG

Dream Defilement

The Emptiers: *Thieves of Darkness, 1* https://a.co/d/5I4n5mc

Evil Touch

Failed Assignment

Fantasy Spirit Spouse https://a.co/d/hW7oYbX

FAT Demons (The): *Breaking Demonic Curses* https://a.co/d/4kP8wV1

The Fold (5-book series)

- The Fold (Book 1)
- Name Your Seed (Book 2)
- The Poor Attitudes of Money (3)
- Do Not Orphan Your Seed (4)
- For the Sake of the Gospel (5)
- My Sowing Journal

Gang Ups: Touch Not God's Anointed

Getting Rid of Evil Spiritual Food

https://a.co/d/i2L3WYQ

got HEALING? Verses for Life

got LOVE? Verses for Life

got HOPE? Verses for Life

got money? https://a.co/d/g2av41N

Here Come the Horns: *Skilled to Destroy*
https://a.co/d/cZiNnkP

Hidden Sins: Hidden Iniquity

https://a.co/d/4Mth0wa

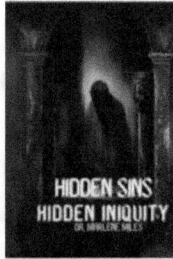

How to Dental Assist

How to Dental Assist2: Be Productive, Not Wasteful

How to STOP Being a Blind Witch or Warlock

I Take It Back

Legacy

Let Me Have A Dollar's Worth
https://a.co/d/h8F8XgE

Level the Playing Field

Living for the NOW of God

Lose My Location
https://a.co/d/crD6mV9

Love Breaks Your Heart

Made Perfect In Love

Mammon https://a.co/d/29yhMG7

Man Safari, *The*

Marriage Ed. Rules of Engagement & Marriage

Made Perfect in Love

Money Hunters: Beware of Those

Money on the Altar https://a.co/d/4EqJ2Nr

Mulberry Tree, *The*
https://a.co/d/9nR9rRb

Motherboard (The) - *Soul Prosperity Series*

Name Your Seed

Occupy: *Until I Return*
https://a.co/d/bZ7ztUy

Plantation Souls

Players Gonna Play

Portals: Shut the Front Door: Prayers to Close Evil Portals.

Power Money: Nine Times the Tithe

https://a.co/d/gRt41gy

The Power to Get Wealth
https://a.co/d/e4ub4Ov

Powers Above

The Robe, Part 1, The Lessons of Joseph

The Robe, Part II, The Lessons of Joseph

Seasons of Grief

Seasons of Waiting

Seasons of War

Second Marriage, Third--, *Any Marriage*

https://a.co/d/6m6GN4N

Seducing Spirits: Idolatry & Whoredoms

https://a.co/d/4Jq4WEs

Shut the Front Door: *Prayers to Close Portals* https://a.co/d/cH4TWJj

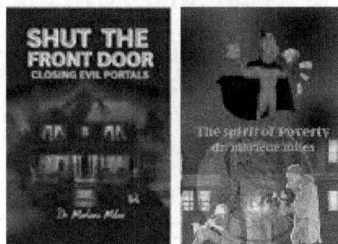

Sift You Like Wheat

Six Men Short: What Has Happened to all the Men?

SLAVE

Soul Prosperity soul prosperity series 3

https://a.co/d/5p8YvCN

Souls Captivity soul prosperity series 2

The Spirit of Anti-Marriage

The Spirit of Poverty
https://a.co/d/abV2o2e

Spiritual Thieves https://a.co/d/eqPPz33

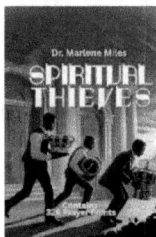

StarStruck- Triangular Power series.

SUNBLOCK- Triangular Power series.

The Swallowers: *Thieves of Darkness,* 3

Take It Back

This Is NOT That: How to Keep Demons from Coming at You

Time Is of the Essence

Too Many Wives: *Why You Have Lady Problems*

Tormenting Spirits
https://a.co/d/dAogEJf

Toxic Souls

Triangular Power *(series)*

- Powers Above
- SUNBLOCK
- Do Not Swear by the Moon
- STARSTRUCK

Unbreak My Heart: *Don't Let Me Die*

Uncontested Doom

Unguarded Hours, *The*

Unseen Life, *The* (forthcoming)

Upgrade: How to Get Out of Survival Mode

- Toxic Souls (Book 2 of series)
- Legacy (Book 3 of series)

The Wasters: *Thieves of Darkness,* Bk 2
https://a.co/d/bUvI9Jo

What Have You to Declare? What Do You Have With You from Where You've Been?

When I Was A Child, *I Prayed As a Child*

When the Devourer is Rebuked

https://a.co/d/1HVv8oq

The Wilderness Romance *(series)* This series is about conducting a Godly relationship and marriage with someone who is a Wilderness person. It is about how to recognize it and navigate through it. These books are about how not to get caught up in such.

- *The Social Wilderness*
- *The Sexual Wilderness*
- *The Spiritual Wilderness*

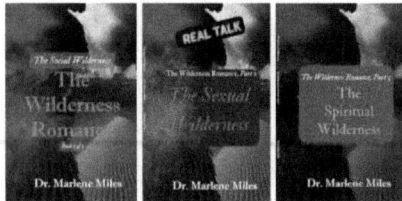

Other Series

The Fold (a series on Godly finances)
https://a.co/d/4hz3unj

Soul Prosperity Series https://a.co/d/bz2M42q

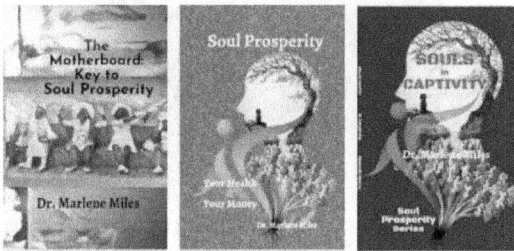

Spirit Spouse books

https://a.co/d/9VehDSo

https://a.co/d/97sKOwm

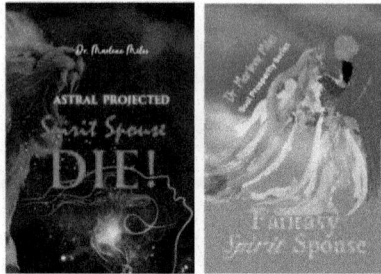

Battlefield of Marriage, The

https://a.co/d/eUDzizO

Players Gonna Play

https://a.co/d/2hzGw3N

Sent Spirit Spouse (can someone send you a spirit spouse? This book is not yet released.)

Matters of the Heart

Made Perfect in Love
https://a.co/d/70MQW3O

Love Breaks Your Heart
https://a.co/d/4KvuQLZ

Unbreak My Heart
https://a.co/d/84ceZ6M

Broken Spirits & Dry Bones
https://a.co/d/e6iedNP

Thieves of Darkness series

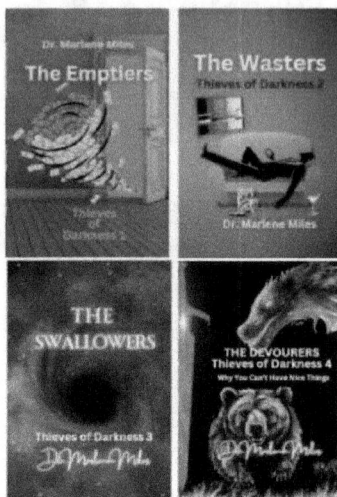

The Emptiers https://a.co/d/heio0dO

The Wasters https://a.co/d/5TG1iNQ

The Swallowers https://a.co/d/1jWhM6G

The Devourers: Why We Can't Have Nice Things https://a.co/d/87Tejbf

Spiritual Thieves

Triangular Powers https://a.co/d/aUCjAWC

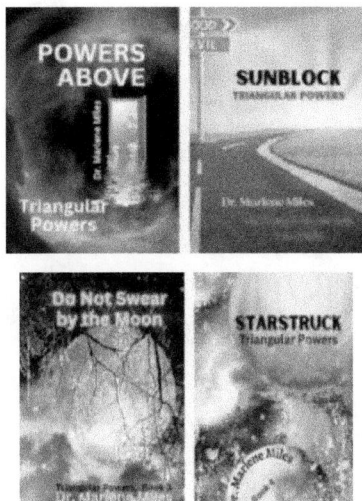

Upgrade (series) *How to Get Out of Survival Mode* https://a.co/d/aTERhXO